ALLIGATORS & CROCODILES

Printed in Hong Kong

98 99 00 01 02 5 4 3 2 1

Library of Congress Cataloging-in-Publication Data
Behler, John L.
    Alligators and crocodiles / John L. Behler and Deborah A. Behler.
       p.   cm. — (World life library)
    Includes bibliographical references and index.
    ISBN 0-89658-370-8
    1. Alligators. 2. Crocodiles. I. Behler, Deborah A. II. Title.
    III. Series.
    QL666.C925B438   1998
    597.98—dc21   97-28583
                                                                        CIP

Distributed in Canada by Raincoast Books, 8680 Cambie Street, Vancouver, B.C. V6P 6M9

Published by Voyageur Press, Inc.
123 North Second Street, P. O. Box 338, Stillwater, MN 55082 U.S.A.
612-430-2210, fax 612-430-2211

Educators, fundraisers, premium and gift buyers, publicists and marketing managers: Looking for creative products and new sales ideas? Voyageur Press books are available at special discounts when purchased in quantities, and special editions can be created to your specifications. For details contact the marketing department at 800-888-9653

Photographs copyright © 1998 by

Front cover © Konrad Wothe (Oxford Scientific Films)
Back cover © Jonathan Scott (Planet Earth Pictures)
Page 1 © Peter Scoones (BBC Natural History Unit)
Page 4 © Gerard Lacz (NHPA)
Page 6 © Images Colour Library
Page 9 © A.N.T. (NHPA)
Page 10 © Chris Ratier (NHPA)
Page 13 © Martin Wendler (NHPA)
Page 14 © Images Colour Library
Page 16 © Niall Benvie
Page 17 © K Ghani (NHPA)
Page 18 © Images Colour Library
Page 21 Top © M & C Denis-Huot (Planet Earth Pictures)
Page 21 Bottom © Frank Krahmer (Planet Earth Pictures)

Page 22 © Brian Kenney (Planet Earth Pictures)
Page 25 © Images Colour Library
Page 26 © Martin Wendler (NHPA)
Page 29 © Bruce Davidson (Oxford Scientific Films)
Page 31 © Mark Deeble & Victoria Stone (Oxford Scientific Films)
Page 32 © Martin Wendler (NHPA)
Page 35 © Images Colour Library
Page 36 © Daniel Heuclin (NHPA)
Page 39 © Richard Kirby (BBC Natural History Unit)
Page 40 © Michael & Patricia Fogden
Page 43 © Daniel Heuclin (NHPA)
Page 44 © Andre Bartschi (Planet Earth Pictures)
Page 47 Top Left © Brian Kenney (Planet Earth Pictures)
Page 47 Top Right © Ken King (Planet Earth Pictures)

Page 47 Bottom Left © Ken Lucas (Planet Earth Pictures)
Page 47 Bottom Right © Ken Lucas (Planet Earth Pictures)
Page 31 © Mark Deeble & Victoria Stone (Oxford Scientific Films)
Page 51 © Anup Shah (BBC Natural History Unit)
Page 52 © Pete Oxford (BBC Natural History Unit)
Page 31 © Mark Deeble & Victoria Stone (Oxford Scientific Films)
Page 56 © A.N.T. (NHPA)
Page 59 © Daniel Heuclin (NHPA)
Page 60 © Images Colour Library
Page 63 © Doug Perrine (Planet Earth Pictures)
Page 65 © Geoff Du Feu (Planet Earth Pictures)
Page 66 © Martin Wendler (NHPA)

ALLIGATORS & CROCODILES

John L. Behler & Deborah A. Behler

Voyageur Press

Contents

Introduction

At nearly 13 ft (4 m) long, she was a monster. The female 'salty' (saltwater crocodile) had been captured in the Fly, the gigantic river system with a 40-mile- (64.3-km-) wide mouth that disgorges much of the 300 in (7.6 m) of annual rainfall in Papua New Guinea's Western district into the sea. It was nesting season at Moitaka, a government crocodilian farm on the outskirts of the capital, Port Moresby, and she had prepared a mound of rotting vegetation and muck 6 ft (1.8 m) across and half that in height near the edge of a small lagoon. A dozen of us circled behind the nest and moved cautiously toward it. John Lever, an Australian who was assisting the Papua New Guinea (PNG) government to develop a crocodilian farming program for indigenous people, had told me about her somewhat mythical mate – Kikori, the Big One. At nearly 18 ft (5.5 m) and 1700 lb (771 kg), he was one of the largest saltwater crocodiles that had ever been captured and measured. Like the female, he'd come from the Fly River and had been flown to Moitaka. I had been told that the pilot had been extremely worried that his unusual cargo, though tightly trussed, would go berserk and tear the plane apart. To allay his fears, the crocodile had been positioned down the center of the plane with a government officer sitting astride the beast and holding a 30-30 carbine aimed at its head, ready to shoot at the very first sign of trouble. Obviously, the crocodile had behaved himself and survived the ordeal.

I was visiting PNG and the crocodile peoples of the Sepik and Fly river drainages as part of a United Nations Development Programme mission. The crocodile peoples live beside the rivers and their culture is intimately tied to the animals there, particularly the crocodiles, which they hunt for food and hides. The UN Programme is designed to protect wild crocodilian populations by integrating the traditional uses of these reptiles into a closely managed hide industry. Along with Lever and ten of his PNG crocodilian men, I had come to see if we could get a look at the Big One.

As we approached, the female, who had been in the water guarding her nest, began to stir. Her mate was nowhere to be seen. Perhaps he was in the lake beyond us. In addition to

A saltwater crocodile bolts a meal in Kakadu, Northern Territories, Australia.

taking a look at the male, Lever wanted to check the nest to see if she had laid eggs and, if they were fertile, to count them. But first, the female had to be restrained. Two of Lever's men challenged the female by slapping long bamboo poles on the water about 20 ft (6 m) from her. The female launched herself entirely out of the water and rapidly closed the distance between them. In a couple of minutes, the men had slipped the heavy rope nooses attached to the front of the bamboo poles over her snout and pulled them taut. Manning the ropes, the men moved in opposite directions to hold her steady.

We quickly approached the nest and Lever told me to keep a sharp eye out for the male as he went to work. I confess I was paying more attention to the rope-bound female 20 ft (6 m) away than to the seemingly empty water in front of us. At Lever's second reminder, I glanced over at the lake and saw two eyes and a snout tip break the water surface about 50 ft (15.2 m) away. The large space between his snout tip and the back of his skull left no doubt that it was the Big One.

'Oh, my heavens, he's there!… In the back of the pool,' I said.

'Watch him!' yelled Lever.

'He's disappeared,' I replied.

'Let's go!'

What happened next has stayed in my mind for 20 years as sharply as if it had happened yesterday. We retreated a dozen paces from the water's edge and turned to see if he would surface again. A second later, he reappeared just below the bank where the female was lying. After a couple of seconds, the female began to roll over rapidly and twist the ropes around herself. Her mate, seeing the action, charged. In an instant he leaped out of the water and grabbed her at the base of her tail just behind her rear legs. Lifting her rear end clear off the ground with his jaws, he tried to haul her back to the water. A tug of war ensued – between man and leviathan. Two of the men dropped their ropes, grabbed bamboo poles, and began walloping the male on his snout. At last, he loosened his grip, slowly backed to the water, and submerged. Much too late, I realized that I had remained riveted to the spot, much too close, with mouth agape. The incredible scene was a flashback to the primeval days when reptiles ruled the Earth.

A saltwater crocodile sits atop her nest, which she has scraped together
from surrounding soil and vegetation. The species is noted for its fierce disposition
and its large size – monster specimens may reach 18-22 ft (6-7 m).

Nile crocodile swimming in white water, Grumeti River, Serengeti National Park, Tanzania.

Lurid accounts of crocodiles and alligators have both fascinated and horrified readers for as long as pen has been put to paper. Some truly monstrous crocodiles and alligators exist today. They are survivors of the Age of Reptiles and, so far, the Age of Man. Some men and women – like the crocodile clans of Papua New Guinea, the Aboriginal people of coastal Northern territories, the Lake Rudolf Turkana, and certain field biologists and zoomen – intimately share their lives with these behemoths. Some of these relationships are by choice, others are imposed at birth.

The Big One, and two other 18-ft (5.5-m) males also caught in the Fly River region, are the largest crocodiles ever recorded in captivity. The other two, Cassius and Gomek, were captured in the late 1960s by Australian George Craig, who operated a general store on Daru Island in the Gulf of Papua. Gomek subsequently was imported into the United States in 1984 by inventor and entrepreneur Arthur Jones. Gomek was the largest crocodile on display in the Western world until his death in 1997.

The maximum lengths and ages of crocodilians are a matter of great controversy. After 'How do you tell them apart?' (see p 20), the most frequently asked questions are 'How big do they get?' and 'How old is it?' There are records of wild crocodilians living more than a century, but they have not been authenticated. There are, however, reliable zoological park records which reveal that captive crocodilians can outlive their keepers. The Cincinnati Zoo's captive American alligator is more than 70 years old. Chinese alligators, taken as adults in the wild, have captive longevities exceeding 50 years. One female Chinese alligator successfully bred for the first time and produced eggs and offspring when she was more than 50 years of age. It appears that crocodiles are not as long-lived as alligators. Yet, environmental conditions and diets have dramatically improved in zoological institutions during the past 25 years, and impressive longevity records will most certainly be set in the coming years for all crocodilian species.

The Guinness Book of Animal Facts and Feats lists the American alligator and the American, the Orinoco, the Nile and the saltwater crocodiles as the largest living reptiles, each of these species having the potential to reach 18 ft (5.5 m) or beyond in length. The longest American alligator on record, collected by E. H. McIlhenny in 1890, was 19 ft 2 in (5.84 m). Today, large male American alligators measure 12 ft (3.6 m) in length, females 9 ft (2.7 m). Specimens greater than 14 ft (4.2 m) are virtually unknown. Of the crocodiles, the 'salty' is the largest, with several reliable modern records exceeding 20 ft (6 m). Their last stronghold is Papua New Guinea. The largest skull on record (29.53 in; 750 mm) is preserved in the Indian Museum collection in Calcutta. It reportedly belonged to a 25-ft (7.6-m) saltwater crocodile that lived in the Hooghly River. The total lengths of living crocodiles can be accurately determined by ratios worked out by biologists studying morphometric relationships for the various species. These have served to dispel many 'records'. On the basis of ratios, this animal measured at least 22 ft (6.7 m) when alive.

Until quite recently, all crocodilians have been loathed as potential man-eaters. That general sense allowed the unregulated take of tens of millions of crocodiles, alligators, caimans, and gharials for their hides. And travelers through crocodilian habitat simply shot the animals as vermin. While crocodilians are indeed the dominant predators in their aquatic world, most species are relatively timid and of little danger to man. It is true, however, that Nile and saltwater crocodiles have been documented as man-eaters. There can be little doubt that they have had a profound impact on cultures living within their ranges, and still do. These species, often featured in TV wildlife documentaries, continue to influence the way we view all crocodilians. Yet education seems to be changing the public's attitude that crocodilians are adversaries that need to be throttled to near extinction.

Protective laws have led to spectacular comebacks for some species such as the American alligator and the saltwater crocodile populations of Australia and Papua New Guinea. These recoveries have, however, coincided with greater human intrusion into their domains. Housing subdivision activity in American alligator habitat has taken place at a frenetic pace. Outdoor recreation has exploded. Fishermen, boaters, golfers, swimmers, campers, dog trainers, and 'wilderness explorers' are all competing for the alligator's space. The vast majority of human-alligator interactions are benign. But when reported to authorities as pests, the alligators always lose. Most often they are removed from their habitat and destroyed. The few legitimate attacks on humans are invariably spawned by reckless behavior. Unfortunately, these serve to polarize our attitudes against crocodilians and reduce our tolerance toward them. In the end, crocodilians may become only curiosities in scattered refuges and parklands.

These black caimans were saved from an
ill-fated Bolivian ranching scheme and are awaiting
transfer to the Beni Biosphere Reserve.

Living Crocodilians of the World

General Characteristics

The 23 living species in the reptilian order Crocodylia inhabit ecosystems throughout the world's tropical and subtropical regions. These 23 species are distributed in three families (or subfamilies by some authorities). There are two alligators and six caiman in the family Alligatoridae. With the exception of the Chinese alligator, these animals are found in the southern United States and central South America. Thirteen crocodile species are currently recognised in the family Crocodylidae. Of the four species inhabiting the American tropics, the American crocodile is the most widespread, ranging from extreme southern Florida to northern South America. Three of the crocodile species live in Africa; the most well-known is the Nile crocodile, which inhabits a wide variety of aquatic regions from the sub-Saharan countries all the way to the tip of South Africa. The remaining six crocodiles are found in southern Asia-Australian waters. The saltwater crocodile has the largest range of all living crocodilians, living throughout the IndoPacific. The last assemblage, the family Gavialidae, includes the true gharial, which inhabits river drainages from Pakistan to Myanmar, and the false gharial, found only on the Malaysian peninsula and nearby islands.

These species designations continue to be debated by experts. The false gharial is often placed in the same family as the true crocodiles, but current information strongly suggests that it is more closely related to the gharial. The classification of crocodilians has traditionally been based on skulls and other skeletal characteristics. In recent years, a wider spectrum of criteria, including internal anatomy and biochemical and genetic comparisons, are being used to assess the relationships among crocodilians. These tools will likely lead to the descriptions of new taxa and a clearer understanding of the relationships of all living crocodilians and their predecessors.

All crocodilians have features in common and their general body plan has changed little in 200 million years. Their excellent design has stood the test of time. They differ from each other in snout proportions and modest skeletal and dental characteristics, and animals

The American alligator has keen eyesight. Worn teeth are replaced by new teeth developing below them.

range in size from 5–20+ ft (1.5–6+ m). Nearly 80% of their body weight is muscle and armored skin. Crocodilians have a four-chambered heart, which enhances the efficiency of blood circulation by separating oxygenated and unoxygenated blood. They also have a diaphragm and a cerebral cortex.

On the external surface, crocodilians are covered with thick skin protected by non-overlapping scales, or scutes, with bony buttons, or osteoderms, embedded in them. These give the scales on the upper surface a keeled appearance and provide their dorsal armor. The scales are richly supplied with blood. When the animal basks, the heated blood is transported into the body. On the belly scales, osteoderms are reduced or absent. This is why the belly skins are most desired for tanning into fine leather products.

American alligator gape and eye.

The crocodilian skull is diapsid, meaning it has two holes behind the eye socket, which serve as attachment sites for muscles. This arrangement facilitates great extension of the jaw muscles. When the jaws of an adult close, they can do so with tremendous force, exerting tons of crushing pressure (and in large crocs they can do so with a crushing force of 3000 lb / 1360 kg per sq in), manyfold greater than man's capability. They can easily crush a turtle shell or a mammal skull. Yet, the muscles that open the jaws are weak. A thick rubber band placed around the jaws of a 6-ft (1.8-m) crocodilian can easily hold them shut. There are no lips to seal the mouth when it closes. Water leaks out the sides but prey items remain entrapped.

The shape of the snout gives a clue to diet. Long, narrow snouts can move quickly in water and enable their owner to snatch passing fish more readily than a broad-snouted crocodilian, which does better at seizing and holding larger mammals. Crocodilian teeth are conical in shape

A mugger crocodile basks in the sun to elevate its body temperature,
which speeds digestion and allows a quick return to feeding.

The eye of an American alligator. The pupil is slit-like in bright sun; at night,
it expands greatly to allow more light to enter the eye. Crocodilians have moveable eyelids
and a transparent third eyelid, which covers the eye when they are submerged.

and are not meant for chewing; rather they are designed to penetrate and hold prey. When the jaws shut the teeth intermesh perfectly. Each tooth is set in a socket in the jaw, rather than being perched on the top or the side of the jaw as we see in lizards, snakes, and the tuatara. Tooth number varies according to species. The gharial, a narrow-snouted crocodilian, has the most teeth – 106 to 110. The American alligator has 80, the Nile crocodile 68. Each tooth has a replacement tooth in place below it. When a worn or damaged tooth is lost, the replacement tooth moves into place. This process continues throughout life. Native Americans once used the teeth from large alligators as powder horns.

Crocodilians have color vision and their eyes are protected by a third eyelid, called the nictitating membrane, which moves sideways across the eyeball when the animal submerges or is involved in a confrontation. Although crocodilians are not believed to have good underwater vision, they have good aerial eyesight. Their eyes are adapted for vision under low light levels. During the day, the iris is reduced to a vertical slit; at night, it is open to a full circle. Under these conditions, the tapedum of the eye will reflect a red shine, which can be seen at great distances when a flashlight beam hits it. The eyes are perched close together above the level of the snout and oriented forward. As a result, crocodilians have 25 degrees of overlap between the right and left eye vision. This binocular vision aids in judging distances.

The senses of hearing and smell also appear well developed. The ears, which readily detect small disturbances in their aquatic environment, are located behind the eyes. Two valve-like folds of skin protect the eardrum. Crocodilians are the only reptiles with earflaps, which close when they submerge or when the nictitating membrane of the eye closes. The nasal passages are complex structures, which suggest that the sense of smell is quite sophisticated. The openings to the nasal passages, via external nostrils, are positioned on a pad of skin at the snout tip. Water is prevented from entering the air tubes, which lead to the back of the throat and the internal nostrils, by flaps of skin that cover the openings when the animal submerges. Of course, crocodilians can breathe through their mouth, too. A huge flap, called the palatal valve, closes the air passageway when necessary, as when the animal is drowning prey. The large fleshy tongue sits in front of the palatal valve and is attached along its length to the arms of the lower jaw. The lingual glands of the tongue are actually salt glands which secrete excess salt when crocodilians are in high saline environments. These structures are well developed in crocodiles, not so much in alligators and caiman. This has given support to the belief that modern crocodiles evolved from marine ancestors and modern alligators from a freshwater ancestry.

The relatively short legs of crocodilians do not support them well when they leave water. If forced to move overland, they assume a 'high walking gait', in which the legs are held erect under their body and the tail drags as they walk. They can move at about 1¼–2½ mph (2–4 kph) but tire quickly and they must rest frequently. Some crocodilians making a mad dash for water assume a galloping gait, which can carry them at about 11 mph (18 kph) for a short distance. Crocodilians are designed for aquatic life. Here, their short legs are appropriately sized so they do not create extra drag while swimming. Then, the legs are folded back along the sides and the body moves in undulating fashion, and the broad, very powerful, laterally compressed tail provides propulsion. Its broad form also comes in handy for excavating water holes in the dry season and for piling up vegetation into a nest mound. The front feet have five unwebbed toes while the rear feet have four toes that are strongly webbed. While the animal is floating, the rear feet are usually splayed, with toes and webbing spread out for stability.

Alligator or Crocodile?

To the untrained eye, all crocodilians look pretty much alike; heavily armored skin, long cylindrical body, long tail, short, stubby legs that look almost too small for the body plan, and enormous jaws with lots of teeth. In fact, it's relatively easy to quickly distinguish alligators from crocodiles… as long as they keep their jaws shut. The enlarged fourth tooth on the lower jaw of the alligator (and its caiman kin) fits neatly into a full socket in the upper jaw and cannot be seen when the mouth is shut. The alligator's snout is also quite broad and relatively short. And the alligator appears black when wet, dark gray when it is dry after basking in the sun.

Crocodiles, by comparison, are typically tan or greenish, have a longer, more slender snout and a snaggle-toothed appearance when their jaws are closed. The fourth tooth juts upward into a notch on the upper jaw and is very clearly seen. If the animal looks as if it is leering at you when its jaws are closed, it's a crocodile.

When a crocodile closes its jaws, the largest tooth on the bottom fits into a notch on the upper jaw and is visible – a trait which distinguishes them from alligators.

Life History

Crocodilians, despite their long evolutionary history, should not be considered primitive creatures. They are the most advanced of all living reptiles. In fact, there is genetic evidence that crocodilians are more closely related to birds than they are to lizards and snakes. The modern crocodilians – alligators, caimans, crocodiles, and gharials – are highly specialized for life in subtropical and tropical rivers, lakes, swamplands, and marshes. For more than 140 million years they have dominated these environments. They are superbly designed predators. Crocodilians have what has been described as 'minimum exposure posture' in water. All their sensory apparatus – eyes, ears, and nostrils – periscopes out of the water, while the great bulk of their body remains hidden below it.

Although the crocodilians differ in size and habitat requirements, their basic biology is similar. They are the largest predators of their aquatic environment. They are nocturnally active, so most of their feeding takes place between dusk and dawn. If prey presents itself during the day, however, they will seize the opportunity to take a meal. Most meals are taken along the shoreline by sit-and-wait predation – the animal simply lies in wait for a disturbance in the water near its jaws and then it snaps at it. Crocodilians will also leap to grab prey moving on vegetation above or even flying overhead. And they may feed underwater on the bottom or stalk distant prey by moving underwater to within easy striking distance.

Temperature strongly influences feeding behavior. These animals feed under warm conditions and fast when it is cool. As juveniles, they mainly eat invertebrates – aquatic insects, snails, crayfish, crabs. Adults graduate to vertebrates and may include snakes, turtles, birds, and mammals in their diet. The largest crocodilians will eat virtually any living thing that ventures within range of their snout, and that includes people and domestic stock. Most crocodilians are really opportunistic feeders, taking whatever prey species are abundant in their environment. Some, however, are specialists, such as the gharial, which eats mainly fish.

Crocodilians are ectothermic as are other reptiles. They are heat seekers and maintain

Hatchling American alligators face a world of predatory fish, reptiles, birds and mammals.

their body temperatures within narrow parameters. Unlike endothermic birds and mammals, which regulate their body temperatures internally, crocodilians do so behaviorally by exploiting the hot zones in their environment. By moving into warm shallows or onto land to bask in the sun, they raise their body temperatures to between 77° and 95° F (25° and 35° C). To cool off, the animals seek shade or move into the water. Being able to thermoregulate effectively is vitally important to the crocodilian's well-being. A body temperature above 81° F (27° C) is needed for digestive enzymes to function well and for energy to be assimilated. At sub-optimal temperatures, food will ferment in the animal's stomach. Thus, wild crocodilians that are feeding display heat-seeking behavior (those that are fasting select lower temperatures to conserve energy). The higher the body temperature, the greater the digestion efficiency, and the faster the animal grows. Injured and ill crocodilians also seek hot zones in their environment. They spend long hours basking, and the high body temperatures they achieve help ward off infection and promote healing. Hatchling crocodilians seek high temperatures, which allow them to digest the large stores of yolk present in their body cavities at birth. The unusually high body temperatures they reach promote rapid growth, exhausting their natal food supply and stimulating early feeding. Only the American alligator and the Chinese alligator remain active at temperatures between 54° and 59° F (12° and 15° C), but they do not eat at these temperatures, which are too low for digestion to take place. For many years, hatchling alligators and caimans have been sold as pets. The vast majority die quickly because their keepers do not understand the basic thermal needs of the animals.

In addition to maintenance behavior such as feeding, temperature regulation, and predator avoidance, crocodilians display diverse and sophisticated social and reproductive behaviors, which include communication, dominance hierarchies, courtship, and maternal behavior. These can be touched upon only lightly here.

Crocodilian social behavior specialist Jeffrey Lang describes crocodilians as the 'loudmouths of the reptile world'. And they start early in life. Communication begins in the nest, before hatching. Late in crocodilian egg development, embryonic sounds in one egg are repeated in neighboring eggs. This likely synchronizes hatching and signals the attendant mother alligator or crocodile that hatching is imminent. Once hatching has occurred, any new experience seems

*Female crocodilians are great mothers. A Nile crocodile female at South Africa's
St. Lucia Estuary carries her hatchlings from nest to water.*

Young basking black caiman. This species is widely distributed in the Amazon River Basin.

to stimulate vocalizations. Adults are especially sensitive to the hatchling and juvenile 'distress calls' and respond aggressively. Young call most frequently when they disperse in the evening to feed and when they come together again in the morning. The 'contact call' serves to reassemble the family unit and keep the crèche intact. They become less vocal as they mature, and some species rarely vocalize. The American alligator is at the extremely noisy end of the spectrum. In alligator country, bellowing choruses of breeding males and females can be heard across the wetlands during the spring breeding season, which is from March to June in North America (from October to December in Australia). However, where the ranges of different crocodilians overlap, their peak breeding season may vary by a month or so, acting as an isolating mechanism to prevent interspecific breeding. The age at which crocodilians are able to reproduce varies, depending upon species, habitat, growth and conditions. Generally the age is between 10 and 15 years, but can be as little as five years in smaller species.

Some of their calls are subtle, however. Courting alligators issue a cough-like, low intensity call, that can be heard only for several yards. Crocodilians also communicate acoustically. The best-known performance in this repertoire is the 'headslap'. An animal will lift its head above the water, with the bottom jaw just visible, and hold that position for a period of time. Then, without warning, it quickly opens its jaws and slams them shut an instant before it smacks them on the surface of the water. The loud pop and crack display is often followed by submersion of the head and blowing of bubbles. The headslap message stimulates similar activity among other crocodilians. It, and bellowing, establish and maintain long-term social relationships.

Social status is also conveyed by body posturing. Lifting the head, back, and tail high out of the water communicates size and dominance information to other crocodilians. Dominant animals swim boldly at the surface, while subordinate individuals swim with just their heads exposed. When approached by a dominant animal, the lesser crocodilian lifts its head high out of the water and exposes its throat to the aggressor, which indicates subordinate rank and perhaps information about sex. Dominant male crocodilians defend territories from which they may exclude other males from their mates, favorite basking sites, feeding stations, their mate's nesting location, and seasonal retreats. The territory ranges are highly variable and depend upon the complexity of habitat, visual barriers and species, but can exceed several hectares.

Female crocodilians typically initiate courtship when they are ready to breed and may move with impunity among territorial males and mate with a number of them. This social interaction follows complex pair formation and precopulatory rituals, including head and body rubbing, vocalizations, bubbling, circling, and riding. These behaviors eventually lead to the male riding on the back of the female. The 'couple' submerges and the male wraps his tail under hers and presses his vent to hers. The male's penis is extruded, enters her vent, and sperm is delivered into her reproductive tract.

Sunny river sandbanks or high ground situations in marshes, swamplands, or lake margins are typical nesting locations. Some crocodilians are hole nesters, others mound nesters. In the former, the female scoops out a suitably sized cavity into which she deposits her clutch of eggs and covers it. The second option is more complicated and requires the female to create a large mound of vegetation, humus, and soil in the center of which she lays her eggs. The number of eggs laid – anywhere from 10 to 70 – depends on the species. The heat generated by the decomposing vegetation will add to that supplied by the sun. Females often remain close to their nests and guard them against predators. If the nests are not predated or ravaged by floods, they produce hatchlings in 60 to 100 or so days, depending on species. Male crocodilians take no part in nest-making.

Crocodilian eggs are hardshelled like those of birds, and the calcareous coat controls water loss. They also have a substantial food supply, the yolk, which provides nourishment during incubation. In birds and mammals, sex is determined at the time of conception. In crocodilians, sex of the individual is determined as the egg matures. Scientists have known for a long time that temperature during incubation affects the growth and development of crocodilian eggs. More recently, they discovered that incubation temperatures during the first few weeks after the egg is laid determine if the animal is male or female (as it does in turtles). This is called temperature-dependent sex determination. Incubation temperatures vary according to nest environment, but all crocodilians incubate their eggs at temperatures from 86–90° F (30–32° C).

Among alligators and caimans, more females are produced at lower temperatures and

An egg tooth, the size of a grain of sand, on this Nile crocodile's snout has shredded its leathery eggshell.

males predominate at the higher ranges. The situation among the species of crocodiles is not as clear-cut nor as well known. Whether a female produces male or female young depends, to some extent, on where she nests. It also depends on prevailing weather conditions during the nesting season. Drought and low rainfall can mean higher, drier temperatures; the converse is true during cool, rainy weather. If all conditions are optimal, the nest will produce equal numbers of males and females; eggs at the top, or warmest portion, of the nest will hatch as males, and those at the bottom will be females.

Not only can weather determine sex of the hatchlings, it can also directly affect hatching success. Abnormally high water levels and tropical storms can swamp even the best laid nest; prolonged droughts can leave the eggs too high and dry. Then there are the predators. Predation of eggs and hatchlings is extremely high — one reason most crocodilians lay fairly large numbers of eggs. Monitor lizards, raccoons, skunks, pigs, storks, and many other animals dig open the nests and eat the eggs. On sandy beaches, even other crocodilians can destroy the nests of others as they dig their own cavities. In many countries, humans eat crocodilian eggs and harvest them from nests for sale in markets.

Even after they hatch, crocodilians face a number of dangers. Most egg predators will also take baby crocs. Other creatures that cannot easily gain access to the nests pursue hatchlings — herons, egrets, birds of prey. In many species of crocodilians, the females deter predators by remaining near their nests during the incubation period, sometimes even lying on top of a mound nest. Once youngsters reach about 3 ft (1 m) in length, at about two to five years, predation is rare.

In South America, large anacondas and jaguars have been observed killing caimans. Hippos and elephants have been known to kill crocodiles, probably in defense of their young. Sometimes, crocodilians can be their own worst enemies. Adults occasionally eat subadults, and subadults will eat juveniles. But parents do not cannibalize their own young. By and large, however, juvenile and adult crocodilians have little to fear from other animals — other than man, that is. If they are fortunate, they will reach sexual maturity in 5 to 15 years and contribute to the next generation of their kind.

Juvenile Nile crocodiles sun themselves along the Grumeti River
on Tanzania's Serengeti Plains. As adults, they will feed on wildebeests
that cross the river during annual migrations.

Alligators & Caimans

The term 'alligator' originated from early Spanish explorers who encountered large lizard-like reptiles in the southeastern United States. They called these creatures *el lagarto* meaning 'lizard'. The Spanish also coined the term 'caiman', from a Carib-Indian word. The eight species of alligators and caimans share several physical characteristics. The most notable is the arrangement of the teeth; the lower set are hidden when the jaws close, and the fourth tooth fits in a special pit in the upper jaw. In addition, the snout is broad and relatively short compared with those of the true crocodiles and the gharials.

The American alligator is one of the best known of all the crocodilians and is a wildlife conservation success story. It has enjoyed remarkable recovery since the days of rampant poaching and unbridled hide-hunting. Over-exploited since the 1800s, the species was declared endangered in the 1960s. Today, its numbers are healthy and it is widely distributed in the southeastern United States.

The ecology and behavior of this species have been so well studied that the alligator, along with the Nile crocodile, is used as a yardstick for other crocodilian research. The record length for the species, recorded in the nineteenth century, exceeds 19 ft (5.8 m), but today big males rarely reach 14 ft (4.3 m). Maximum size for females is between 9 and 10 ft (2.7 and 3 m). Juvenile alligators are generally black with yellowish or cream crossbands that gradually become less distinct as the animal grows. Dry, basking animals have a uniform dark gray appearance. The studies by crocodilian authorities Jeff Lang, Les Garrick, Howard Hunt, Myrn Watanabe, and Kent Vliet on American alligator courtship, social displays, vocalizations, nesting behavior, and parental care of the young have dramatically increased our understanding of this remarkable carnivore.

Sexual maturity is both age and size dependent. The females reach sexual maturity at about 6.5 ft (2 m) and between 6 and 10 years old. They are courted and mate in April or May, after they emerge from hibernation. Males and females communicate through head slaps and

Broad-snouted caiman hatchlings may remain in the protective care of their mother for more than a year.

bellows. They also make throaty sounds too low-pitched for humans to hear. These intense sounds agitate the water around the animals and create what has been dubbed the 'water dance'. Before mating, male and female alligators touch and bump each other in a slow courtship ritual. In June or July, the female constructs a mound nest of vegetation, lays her clutch of eggs in a cavity in the center of the nest, and then covers them to incubate for about 65 days. She stays near the nest site, guarding her eggs from raccoons and other predators. When she hears the hatchlings grunting in the nest, she digs them out and carries them in her jaws to water. In some cases, the hatchlings overwinter with the female in a den. In areas of low disturbance, the young may remain with the female for two to three years.

When settlers first colonized the southeastern United States, American alligators were plentiful in rivers, swamps, and other waterways. Commercial slaughter of American alligators for their skins to make leather bags, belts, shoes and boots and other items reached its peak after the Civil War and continued into the early 1900s. By the 1950s and early 60s, tanneries had turned to exotic species because the numbers of American alligators had been depleted. National and international protective measures introduced in the late 1960s and the 70s allowed the species to recover, and it did so rapidly. Today, many alligator populations are healthy, so much so that in some heavily populated areas the reptiles have become pests, and nuisance alligator programs have been established to manage these animals. Commercial ranching and farming operations are active in Florida and Louisiana and the alligator skin industry is well regulated. It generates more than $10 million annually, thus providing an incentive to retain habitat and tolerate the alligators' presence in rural areas.

The outlook for the Chinese alligator is not nearly so promising as that for the American alligator with which it shares the genus *Alligator*. The Chinese 'gator is one of the world's most critically endangered crocodilians. Its range today is restricted to a fraction of its former distribution in the Yangtze River system habitat – primarily modified wetlands in agricultural and tree farming communes – in Anhui and Zhenjiang provinces. There it is found mainly in 26 tiny protected areas in the Anhui Research Center of Chinese Alligator Reproduction Conservation Reserve (ARCCAR) and a few localities outside the reserve in Anhui Province. Habitat destruction and intense human competition are the principal causes of the animal's plight.

With nostrils and eyes periscoped above the water, an American alligator moves undetected toward prey.

A dwarf caiman grabs a large meal along a small stream deep in the Amazonian rain forest.
This is the smallest of the crocodilian species, reaching no more than 4 ft (1.2 m).

The Chinese alligator looks like a miniature version of its American counterpart and is about half its size, with a maximum length of 7 ft (2.2 m). Because of the temperate climate, the Chinese alligator spends much of the colder months in burrows it digs in banks on the edges of wetlands. Some of these dens are quite extensive and may have more than one entrance, underground pools, and 20 or more 'rooms'. The burrows may be used by more than one alligator, but, other than a female with offspring, the relationship of these animals is not known. Mating begins in June, a month after the start of the rainy season. Social behavior of the Chinese alligator is similar to that of the American alligator. Animals bellow to communicate their location. Females nest in July and hatchlings emerge in September, after an incubation period of about 70 days. Like her American cousin, the female liberates her young from the nest and carries them to the water. By October, the alligators seek the shelter of their dens.

Chinese alligators have suffered from pollution, dam construction, conversion of wetland habitats to farms, and man's intolerance. Researchers estimate that over the past 20 years the species' range has shrunk by 90%. The current wild population has been estimated at 800 to 1000 animals. The Chinese alligator is protected by national and international law, but people kill them as dyke-destroying pests or sell them to zoos or government-sponsored farms. A farming scheme started in 1979 stimulated the collection of breeding stock from the wild. More than 200 specimens were captured. These animals produced 4000 young by 1991, but none of these animals has been returned to the wild. In 1992, ARCCAR registered with CITES as a captive breeding farm and qualified to enter the commercial trade. China's intention was to sell alligator meat locally and to send small Chinese alligators to Europe for the exotic pet markets. None of these plans, and others advanced since then, seem to be directed toward the conservation of the Chinese alligator in nature. Outside China, a successful captive-breeding program was established in 1976 at the Rockefeller Wildlife Refuge in Louisiana, with animals from the Wildlife Conservation Society's Bronx Zoo and the National Zoological Park. As a result of this and subsequent programs in other institutions, more than 200 Chinese alligators are now in captivity outside China.

Among the caimans and, indeed, all the New World crocodilians, the spectacled caiman has the widest range. Although the taxonomy of the spectacled caiman is debated by authorities, two or three subspecies are currently recognized: the nominate form, *Caiman c. crocodilus*, is found throughout the Orinoco drainage in Venezuela and in the Amazon drainage from Colombia southward through Brazil into Peru; *C. c. fuscus* ranges through the Atlantic coastal drainages of Colombia into western Venezuela; and *C. c. chiapasius* (which many experts recognize as *C. c. fuscus*) ranges from southern Mexico to Pacific Colombia. These animals are small to medium in size, and few specimens exceed 8 ft (2.5 m) in length. Aptly named, they have a distinctive bony ridge, or 'spectacle', in front of the eyes. Spectacled caimans are extremely adaptable to rivers, savannas, swamps, lakes, and man-made ponds. In many areas where American crocodiles and black caimans have been hunted out, spectacled caimans have moved into their habitats, now dominate them, and seem to be a negative factor in the recovery of the larger crocodilian species. Liberated pet caimans have established themselves in water-control ditches and borrow pits in the Miami, Florida area, where they appear to compete with resident alligators and drive them out. The caimans mature at smaller than 4 ft (3 m) in four to six years. In South America, their nests are frequently raided by large tegu lizards. In the dry season, large numbers of caimans may congregate at the remaining small water pools. Here, they are commonly taken by anacondas or they may become the meal of a larger caiman.

Historically, caiman skins were considered inferior by hide-hunters, because they have well developed bony buttons on the belly. Consequently, commercial exploitation did not begin until populations of the more valuable species of crocodilians became overhunted and were protected by law. Spectacled caimans, because of their relatively quick generation time and large clutch size, and their ill-tempered personality, have the potential for rapid recovery of population numbers. In many areas they appear to be doing well. Illegal hunting and habitat degradation are concerns, however. Especially discouraging are the study results of Peter Brazaitis, Wildlife Conservation Society crocodile specialist, who has shown through his work with Brazilian biologists that caimans are vanishing at an alarming rate in a broad area across northern Brazil as a consequence of poaching for food, and the toxic effects of lead and mercury poisoning from gold mining operations and industrial waste.

During the dry season, spectacled caimans congregate in a drying pool, where competition is fierce.

Until recently, the yacare caiman was considered to be a subspecies of the spectacled caiman. In appearance, behavior, and ecology, the two species are very similar. Widespread hunting in the 1970s and 80s dramatically reduced their numbers throughout their range, and poaching continues. As with the spectacled caiman, the yacare is adaptable and resilient to hunting pressure.

The yacare caiman shares much of its range with the aptly named broad-snouted caiman which is easily distinguished by its proportionally wide snout — the widest of any crocodilian. The species is flexible in its habitat requirements but prefers shallow, freshwater swamps, the edges of lakes and slow-moving rivers, and mangroves. Where the yacare occurs, Federico Medem, the late patron of South American crocodilian study, found that the broad-snouted caiman sought out more densely vegetated, quieter waters. And in some areas, broad-snouts have adapted to man-made cattle stock ponds. Little is known of the species' natural history and ecology, and much of what is known of their reproductive biology comes from captivity situations where they breed very well. Second-generation hatchings have been recorded at the Bronx Zoo in New York, Atagawa Alligator Farm in Japan, and the University of Sao Paulo in Brazil. As other caimans, the females are mound nesters and lay their eggs during the wet season. The broad-snouted caiman feeds on a wide variety of items, and in some parts of its range, snails are the staple food in its diet. In Argentina and Paraguay most of the species' original habitat remains and healthy populations have been found. Elsewhere, habitat loss is a serious problem and populations have been depleted.

The giant among caimans, indeed of the alligator family, is the black caiman, which can attain a length of 20 ft (6 m). It is an especially handsome animal. Unlike most crocodilians, which are vividly marked as juveniles and become more drab as adults, this species retains its distinctive colors as it matures. Hatchling black caimans have light gray heads with bold, black blotching on the jaws and black bodies with lines of white dots along their sides. In the adult, the head turns brown and the white fades but the colors remain striking. The black caiman is a denizen of flooded savannas, lagoons, oxbows, and quiet river backwaters. It is believed that the black caiman is a keystone species in its environment and plays an important role in maintaining the

The black caiman is the largest member of the alligator family.

stability of the food chain by recycling nutrients to the bottom of the food chain. Fishermen report that when black caimans disappear, there are fewer fish to eat.

The black caiman is an endangered species and it is reported to be severely depleted throughout its range in the Amazon River basin and the Guianas. The invasion of the spectacled caiman into habitat dominated by black caiman appears to be slowing the species' recovery. Poaching, habitat destruction, and mining activities (see p38) continue to be significant threats to its survival. Stronghold populations live in Manu National Park in Peru, Limon Cocha in Ecuador, and Kaw in French Guiana.

Smallest of all the crocodilians, the dwarf caiman averages less than 4 ft (1.2 m) in length. It also is the most primitive of the caimans and is the most heavily armored crocodilian. Its hide is virtually worthless commercially. Unlike other caiman, the dwarf caiman and its cousin the smooth-fronted caiman lack the bony ridges around the eyes and across the snout. Hence they are known collectively as the 'smooth-fronted' caimans, in the genus *Paleosuchus*. Hatchling dwarf caimans have a yellowish-brown skull table which turns rusty after six or so months. Their ear coverlets match the reddish brown top of the head. In the Amazon Basin, the dwarf caiman lives in flooded forests near major rivers and lakes and gallery forest streams in Venezuela. Subsistence hunting is localized and limited numbers are collected for the exotic pet market.

The two *Paleosuchus* look much the same, but the smooth-front is somewhat larger and can be distinguished by the black stripe down the middle of the snout and the black or dark brown ear coverlets that contrast with the lighter skull cap. Habitat of this species is typically streams and small rivers in closed-canopy rainforest. Adults may seek shelter in hollow logs or under debris some distance from water and studies have revealed that they eat a large number of terrestrial vertebrates.

The nesting habits of this species are unusual. Many females build their nests next to a termite mound. Because little sun reaches the floor of their habitat, they take advantage of the stable metabolic heat source of the termite mound to incubate their eggs above 88° F (31° C). The incubation period is the longest recorded for any crocodilian – 100-plus days.

A dwarf caiman beside a pool in Guyana's rain forest. This is the most primitive species of crocodilian.

Crocodiles

New World

Four species of crocodiles live in the tropics of the New World, from the coast of southern Florida to northern South America. None of them are common today, having been decimated by habitat alteration and by hide hunting. In addition, crocodiles suffer from competition for dwindling resources with caimans, which are more adaptable to human disturbance.

Few people realize that there is a crocodile that lives in the United States. Appropriately named, the American crocodile is found in 17 countries from the southern tip of Florida to northern South America. Although it is the most widespread New World crocodile, its numbers have been reduced by four decades (1930s–60s) of commercial exploitation. It is typically a medium size crocodilian, ranging from 10 to 12 ft (3 to 3.6 m), but has the potential to reach a length of 20 ft (6 m). The American crocodile has the most reduced and asymmetrical armor (bony elements in the scales) of any crocodilian and has a prominent hump on the snout between the eyes and nostrils. Its habitats include freshwater and brackish coastal rivers, mangrove swamps, lagoons, and estuaries. The American crocodile was once fairly common in the Everglades and the Florida Keys, but its U.S. population fell from an estimated high of 2000 to as low as 100 to 400 animals because of habitat loss, commercial hunting and killing as pests, and collisions with automobiles. Under protection of the U.S. Endangered Species Act, the numbers of American crocodiles appear to have increased in Florida in recent years. Current threats are continued hunting and habitat degradation. In some areas it appears that the spectacled caiman, an aggressive colonizer, is another factor preventing this species' recovery.

The Orinoco crocodile was once found throughout the streams and seasonally flooded llanos of the Orinoco River basin, but hunting for its hide during the 1930s through the 1960s decimated the populations. Though commercial hunters soon turned to other species of crocodilians, the Orinoco croc has never recovered. Today, this species continues to suffer from illegal hunting and habitat destruction. It is recognized as one of the world's most threatened

American crocodile hatching, Venezuela. Crocodilians begin vocalizing while still in the egg.

reptiles and is listed as Critically Endangered by crocodile specialists. It is seen only in the most remote areas of the middle and lower reaches of the Orinoco. Recently, a survey was launched in Colombia, and field surveys by John Thorbjarnarson and colleagues in Venezuela have revealed small, local populations. Captive-breeding efforts seem to be this species' best hope. Political problems have interfered with programs in Venezuela's Capanaparo River region, but the situation appears to be stabilizing there.

Morelet's crocodile, a freshwater crocodile of northern Central America, prefers marshes, swamplands, and lagoons but it is found in brackish situations in some areas. In the southern part of its range it overlaps with the American crocodile, but the habitat relationships here are not well understood. As other New World crocodiles, Morelet's was decimated by uncontrolled harvest in the 1940s and 50s. The species is protected by law in all three countries where it occurs – Mexico, Guatemala and Belize. While illegal hunting and habitat destruction continue throughout the species' range, some healthy populations exist in each country and interest in survey work and resource management is developing. The species has bred readily in captivity at Tuxtla Gutierrez (Mexico) and Atlanta zoos. In studying maternal behavior at Atlanta, Howard Hunt found that females respond to hatchling vocalizations, open the nest to liberate hatchlings, and will defend them from older Morelet's crocodiles.

The Cuban crocodile has the smallest range of any living crocodilian. It was once widely distributed on the island of Cuba, but today it is found only in the freshwaters of Zapata Swamp in the southwest. A separate population lives in Lanier Swamp on the Isle of Pines. The Cuban croc is yellow-green in color with dark green or black speckling. It is perhaps the most striking crocodilian. It is relatively stocky, very powerfully built and has a massive head and jaws. This croc is an especially good jumper and can 'porpoise' out of a pool to a surprising height. It is an aggressive species, and captive adult specimens are extremely dangerous and untrustworthy. In Cuba, where it has been kept in captivity with American crocodiles, the Cuban is always the dominant species. The two forms readily hybridize in captivity, but behavioral isolating mechanisms appear to keep them apart in nature, despite their overlapping habitats. The number of remaining wild Cuban crocs has been estimated at 3000–6000, and thousands of reproducing captives are in Cuban crocodile farms. A Species Survival Plan program, led by William McMahan

False gharial

African dwarf crocodile

Chinese alligator

Cuban crocodile

at Louisville Zoo, manages the more than 50 Cuban crocodiles in North American zoological park collections.

Africa

There are three crocodiles in Africa. Both the slender-snouted and the dwarf live in the western and central region. The Nile crocodile of Africa and Madagascar is more wide spread and probably the best known of all the crocodile species in the world.

The first modern monograph of ecological study on a crocodilian was written on this species by crocodilian authority Hugh Cott. He showed that there was a dietary shift from juveniles, which primarily eat insects and aquatic invertebrates, to adults, which take mostly vertebrate prey. This is generally true of medium and large crocodilians. The Nile crocodile lives primarily in lakes, rivers, and freshwater swamps where fish, often those species that are predatory on fish species preferred by man, are their major food item. Exceptionally large adult male Nile crocs may exceed 16 ft (4.8 m) in length and are capable of taking large mammal prey. The smaller female becomes sexually mature at 12 to 15 years of age and at about 8 ft (2.4 m) in length. Her eggs are deposited in a sand bank and take 80 to 95 days to hatch. Like the American alligator, the female Nile rarely leaves the nest site. When prompted by calls from the nestlings, she digs open the nest, picks up and holds her young in her gular throat pouch, and takes them to a nursery area in the water. The female may even gently break open eggs that have not hatched yet to release the young. Both parents defend their creche of young for some weeks after they have hatched. Nile females have been reported to nest in the same spot year after year.

The Nile crocodile is highly prized for its hide, and unregulated hunting, as well as indiscriminate killing and habitat destruction from the 1940s to the 60s, completely wiped out some populations and severely depleted others. Protection by national and international laws, and sound management practices, have helped the species' recovery in some regions, particularly in east and south Africa.

As with other crocodilians, the Nile crocodile is a master swimmer and able to carefully control its buoyancy.

The status of the medium-sized, slender-snouted crocodile is in question. It appears to be declining as a consequence of increased hide hunting following the decline of the Nile crocodile, as well as subsistence hunting and habitat destruction. The largest remaining population appears to live along the Ogoue River in Gabon. There are, however, vast areas of potential habitat that remain to be censused in the Democratic Republic of Congo, Niger, and other large river drainages of this politically unstable region. Until recently, little biological information was available on this species. The slender-snouted crocodile is secretive and lives along densely vegetated streams.

Little is known of the ecology of the dwarf crocodile. It is a secretive, nocturnal, and shy animal that avoids large water courses. Its relatively solitary lifestyle, coupled with its restricted daytime activity, small size, and heavily armored bony skin, have saved it from the heavy exploitation experienced by other African crocodiles. It prefers swamp forests and swamp pools and may make extensive voyages on land at night following downpours. It has been reported to use burrows in both the wet and dry seasons. Wild females nest in the wet season and lay small clutches of eggs (average ten), which require 100 days for incubation. Specimens from the upper area of the Democratic Republic of Congo are distinctly different from those elsewhere in the range and were once described as a distinct species. They are now considered to be a subspecies but additional taxonomic work remains to be done.

Asia

Asia boasts the greatest number of crocodile species, with six. They vary from the large estuarine or saltwater crocodile to the much smaller and rarer Philippine crocodile.

The most impressive of the living crocodiles, the saltwater crocodile, still grows to enormous proportions in remote parts of its range. The 'salty' has the largest range of all the crocodilians – from the east coast of India throughout Southeast Asia to the Philippines, New Guinea, and northern Australia. It has been seen far out to sea and has colonized the Solomons and Vanuatu. Although there have been unsubstantiated tales of 26- to 33-ft (8- to 10-m) monsters in earlier days, these can be dismissed for lack of evidence. Still, recent records of 18 to 20 ft (5.5 to 6 m) lengths and one ton weights are awe-inspiring. The saltwater has the

Large crocodiles prey on large quarry. Zebras and gazelles that visit water holes risk being attacked by a hungry Nile crocodile, a highly efficient predator.

Crocodilians communicate their dominance by
headslapping the surface of the water — sometimes several times
in rapid succession — and thrashing their tails about.

reputation of being a man-eater, as does the Nile. The large size and fearsome disposition of the saltwater makes it a formidable creature. There are gruesome accounts of attacks associated with World War II battles in the Bay of Bengal and more recently with boat disasters. In New Guinea, crocodile clans protect the large, old man-eaters, as they believe they carry the souls of their ancestors lost to crocodiles. One 'salty' in Australia's Northern Territory, dubbed 'Sweetheart', achieved celebrity status after attacking small fishing boats and crunching the outboard engines. The disturbance and warmth of the engine may have confused the beast into thinking it was prey. The lesson here is that large saltwater crocodiles can be extremely dangerous and aggressive predators. But as with sharks, most attacks on humans by crocodiles and alligators are not premeditated. They usually occur when people enter the animals' territory, particularly during the mating and nesting season, and act foolishly.

As the common name implies, this crocodile inhabits brackish coastal areas and tidal regions of rivers as well as large freshwater marshes and upper riverine sections. This sea-going species can even survive in the open ocean and has the most efficient salt-excreting glands of any crocodilian. Associated with the tongue, these glands rid the body of excess salt. The female saltwater matures at about 7 to 8 ft (2.2 to 2.5 m) and 12 years of age. As in other crocodiles, the females are considerably smaller in length and mass than their male counterparts. Large females lay big clutches of 40 to 60 eggs. Nesting occurs during the rainy season and many nests can be lost to flooding. Monitor lizards and local peoples dig up the eggs and eat them. Fertile eggs that survive predation and the ravages of nature hatch in about 90 days. Habitat destruction and hunting for its valuable hide took a great toll on most populations of this species. During the 1970s, sound management schemes were developed in Australia and Papua New Guinea and today, their numbers have rebounded from a low of 7500 in Australia to about 100,000 in that country alone.

The mugger crocodile of India and the surrounding area has the broadest snout of all the true crocodiles. During courtship, male muggers have been observed to open their jaws wide and smack them on the surface of the water, clamping them shut on impact to make a hollow noise that resounds for some distance, presumably to advertize their presence and to attract females. They live in freshwater lakes, rivers, and marshes. Nesting takes place in the annual dry season and during the incubation period of 55 to 75 days, mugger females guard their nests from predators, particularly monitor lizards, mongooses, and birds of prey. Well-fed muggers at the Crocodile Bank in Madras, India, lay two clutches of eggs a season. There are more than 10,000 muggers in captivity and there is an overcrowding crisis. A captive-breeding-for-reintroduction project was initiated in 1975. Between 1978 and 1992, more than 1000 offspring from the program were released. Unfortunately, the local peoples remain intolerant and the habitat continues to degrade. The Indian government ordered breeding centers to stop production and the conservation program for this species seems to be at a standstill.

Critically endangered, the Siamese crocodile of mainland south-east Asia has been driven from its habitat by intolerant people who have wantonly killed them and severely disturbed the freshwater swamps, lakes, and slow-moving rivers where they were once found. Today, Siamese crocodiles survive primarily in commercial crocodile farms, where they often hybridize with saltwater crocodiles that share their pools. The ecology of this species and its role as a keystone species in nature is virtually unknown. Its only hope for survival in the wild is the re-establishment of captive-raised stock in strictly protected preserves, local conservation education, and the development of meaningful crocodilian management strategies in the region.

Found only in New Guinea (the world's fourth largest island), the New Guinea crocodile lives throughout the island's huge freshwater marsh, swamp, and riverine complexes. It is a medium-size crocodilian. In the largest of rivers, particularly the Fly and the Sepik, the New Guinea 'freshie' yields ground to the most dominant predator of the region, the saltwater croc, which ventures far upstream of the river's mouth. Experts believe there are two distinct New Guinea croc populations: the northern, which makes nests on floating mats of vegetation during the dry season and lays larger clutches of smaller eggs, and the southern, which nests in the wet season and more often on land. Anatomical differences between these populations have been described. Commercial hunting in past years greatly reduced numbers. Today the crocodiles are managed for sustained harvest, which provides economic incentive to the indigenous peoples sharing their habitat.

The Philippine crocodile, once thought to be a subspecies of the New Guinea croc, is probably the most severely threatened crocodile in the world. Population surveys in the 1980s

A hatchling Nile crocodile basks on its mother's foot. Growth to adulthood may take ten or more years.

An Australian 'freshie' hauls out onto a favorite basking site in a deep billabong.
Its narrow jaws are adept at capturing fish and crustaceans.

indicated that only 500 to 1000 remained in its small range of the Philippines. Few survivors exist in the wild today. Initially they were reduced by hide hunters, but the crocodiles have not been able to recover because of the soaring human population and associated habitat destruction, and killing by intolerant local people. The immediate future for this species looks bleak. Small, but successful captive breeding programs are in place at Silliman University in the Philippines and at the Gladys Porter Zoo in Brownsville, Texas. The Crocodile Farming Institute, operated jointly by the Philippines and Japanese governments, acquired more than 200 specimens from wild and captive sources between 1987 and 1992. Although reproduction has occurred, the farm's contributions to the species' conservation are not clear.

The Australian freshwater crocodile, or 'freshy', is a medium-size species that is quickly recognized by its very slender snout with closely-matched teeth that interface like a pair of opposing sawblades. Its freshwater habitat includes billabongs, swamps, rivers, and floodplain lakes. It ventures into saline environments but does not appear to be able to colonize them because of the more dominate saltwater crocodile living in tidal wetlands. Although severely depleted in numbers as a consequence of uncontrolled hunting during the mid twentieth century, the freshy has recovered in most areas and it is now a well-managed resource.

Gharials

The evolutionary relationship of the gharial and the false gharial has been much debated in scientific circles. Traditionally, the false gharial has been placed in the family Crocodylidae, because its morphology appeared more closely aligned with that of true crocodiles. Recent biochemical, immunological, and cutting-edge DNA studies, however, suggest that the false gharial belongs in the gharial family, Gavialidae. Both gharials, or gavials as they are sometimes called, are found in Asia.

Probably the most distinctive looking of all crocodilians is the extremely narrow-snouted gharial. This large species rivals the saltwater croc in size. Mature males can attain lengths over 20 ft (6 m). At about 13 ft (4 m), the male gharial develops a bulbous appendage on the end of its snout. This structure is said to resemble an Indian pot called a ghara, hence the animal's common name. The function of this nasal appendage is not well known, but it may be a visual indicator of the animal's sex, a sound resonator, or of some other use associated with sexual behavior. The species is the most aquatic crocodilian and does not seem to have the ability to walk in the upright stance that other crocs assume when moving out of water. Gharials appear to prefer deep pools in large rivers.

Females don't become sexually mature until they are nearly 10 ft (3 m) at around 10 to 15 years of age. They nest during the dry season in holes dug in high sand banks along the river's edge. Their eggs are the largest of all the crocodilian eggs. The females do not aid their young in hatching nor do they appear to carry the hatchlings to the safety of water – probably because their long snouts are too slender and delicate. But post-natal care of the young has been observed. Gharials were once common from the Indus River in Pakistan to the Irrawaddy in Burma and south to the Mahanadi in India. As a result of overhunting, habitat destruction, and competition for its main food – fish – the gharial was reduced to an estimated 300 animals in the mid 1970s. Captive breeding and restocking programs in India and Nepal have literally brought this species back from the edge of extinction. The current wild population is believed to exceed 1500 individuals in India, of which 1000 are found in Chambal. In Nepal, only remnant populations remain, and the number may not exceed 100 animals. In Pakistan, Bangladesh, Myanmar and Bhutan, populations are extremely low or have been extirpated. Despite significant conservation efforts, the gharial remains an endangered species.

The false gharial, like the true gharial, is a large crocodilian, and the two species superficially look alike. Male false gharials reach impressive dimensions and may exceed 15 ft (4.6 m), while females are more diminutive in size. The species has a distinctive narrow snout and black bars and bands on its jaws, body and tail. It ranges from Thailand through Malaysia and Borneo and lives in freshwater swamps, lakes, and rivers and is reported to use burrows. Very little is known of its habits in the wild. Females reach sexual maturity at about 9 ft (2.7 m) and nest once a year. Although they have bred at the Bronx and Miami zoos, they have not bred readily in most captive situations. The false gharial is an endangered species and appears to be severely depleted over much of its range as a consequence of deforestation, dam construction, and loss in fish nets.

The gharial is the most aquatic and longest-snouted of all the crocodilians.

Conservation

Crocodilians have been on Earth for a very long time. They date back to the archosaurs, the 'ruling reptiles' that appear in the fossil record of the Upper Triassic period some 200 million years ago. This was a time when other important reptile groups – turtles and lizards – were coming into prominence. The crocodilians were around to witness the arrival of the great dinosaurs, most likely preyed upon them, and survived the global catastrophe that drove many of the spectacular ancient reptiles to extinction at the end of the Cretaceous period, 65 million years ago.

Today, the crocodilians are among the largest animals on Earth. They are the top ranked predators in the food chains of their tropical wetland environments. Their biotic community is fueled by the nutrients in their feces, which are recycled into the foundation elements of the food chain. Removal of crocodilians and the nutrients they leave behind may lead to the decline of other organisms, including fish. This is especially true for nutrient-poor rainforest waters. Very likely crocodilians are a keystone species – a species that determines the structure of their community. When the keystone is lost, biodiversity in the community greatly suffers.

The Alligator Hole

In Africa and Asia, elephants are keystone species that affect their ecosystems by toppling and pulling up trees to create forest gaps, which foster microhabitats for other animals to exploit. When elephants are killed, the complexion of their natural community changes.

Crocodilians play similar roles in their environments. To escape both weather and predators, these reptiles excavate deep holes and burrows in the earth. Their trails through wetland keep watercourses open, and crocodilians enlarge and deepen water holes for resident wildlife during droughts. The American alligator is the master environmental engineer of its ecosystem. In the Everglades of Florida and in other southern marshlands, for example, during the dry season and periodic droughts, the alligator digs depressions into the muck of the marsh with its strong muscled tail, snout and feet. These alligator holes become, in effect, small ponds and may

The American alligator is at home in streams, spring runs, lakes, marshes, canals and even golf-course ponds.

span more than 20 ft (6 m). Rotting plants and mud piled around the holes soon support lush growth. In time, the alligator hole may become the center of an island of trees. These water holes provide sanctuary not only for the alligator but for many aquatic animals, such as snails, fish and turtles, which might otherwise die.

The web of life in a typical alligator hole begins with the periphyton – algae and other tiny organisms – that are eaten by aquatic insect larvae, tadpoles, and small fish. These creatures, in turn, provide food for other larger fish and frogs, which are fed upon by even bigger fish; egrets and other birds; raccoons and other small mammals; and reptiles, such as the alligator itself.

When the rains return, the life that has been preserved in the alligator holes provides the seed stock for repopulating the rejuvenated marshlands. Very appropriately, the American alligator has been described as the keeper of the 'Glades.

The 1960s and 70s were the worst of times for crocodilians. After several decades of unregulated commercial harvest, populations around the world crashed. An estimated 5 to 10 million crocodilians entered the world leather trade each year during the 1950s. Crocodiles and alligators were considered vermin and thought to be in inexhaustible supply. The large crocodile species, and the American alligator, were recognized for their superior quality skins and disappeared first. The market then turned to the bony, less desirable skins of the caimans of South America. By the late 1960s, the supply of available crocodilian skins plummeted. Many skin tanners and cutters went out of business. The larger ones held on, mostly dealing in illegal skins, which drove endangered crocodilians closer to the brink of extinction. The big consumers, the United States and Europe, left the problem in the hands of the crocodilian-producing countries, contending that it was their responsibility to protect their own wildlife. Many, but not all, African and South American countries passed protective laws during the 1960s. However, poachers evaded the lawmakers by smuggling their croc hides to neighboring countries which didn't have such laws and then freely supplied them to the international markets.

In 1969, the United States took a dramatic step to conserve endangered species by amending the Lacey Act, which was passed in 1900 to control the commercial wildlife trade by regulating the market. Originally covering birds and mammals, the Act was amended to include reptiles, amphibians, and fishes. It prohibited the interstate commerce of species harvested or

Top predator of its aquatic habitat, the American alligator plays an important ecological role in recycling nutrients. They also engineer habitats by creating 'gator holes and by keeping trails and waterways open.

exported illegally from their state of origin. It provided the foundation for the United States Endangered Species Act of 1969, which first granted federal protection to the American alligator, precipitating that species' eventual, spectacular recovery. The Act also mandated that the U.S. convene an international conference to draft an endangered species treaty. That conference took place in 1973, and the 81 nations that were present drafted the Convention on International Trade in Endangered Species of Wild Fauna and Flora (CITES). Signatory nations now number more than a hundred. Under CITES, consumer countries agree to share responsibility with producer countries by denying the importation of illegal wildlife and their products. Species endangered by trade are recognized on Appendix I of CITES and their commercial trade is prohibited. Species that could become endangered if their trade were not carefully regulated are placed on Appendix II. Signatory nations that harvest Appendix II species are required to determine that the level of trade allowed will not jeopardize a given species' survival and to limit the number of export permits so that an Appendix II species doesn't become a candidate for Appendix I listing. All 23 species of crocodiles, alligators, caimans, and gharials have been placed on Appendix I or II of CITES in recognition of their many years of unregulated harvest and consequential degraded status (see p 71).

There is no doubt that endangered species legislation, implementation of well-conceived management plans, public education, and CITES have played a major role in turning the tide for many crocodilian populations. Recovery of the American alligator in the southeastern United States, the saltwater crocodile in Australia and Papua New Guinea, and the Nile crocodile in eastern and southern Africa are dramatic success stories. Not all crocodilians, however, have recovered from the days of indiscriminate killing. Today, four species – the Chinese alligator, the Philippine crocodile, the Siamese crocodile, and the Orinoco crocodile – are considered 'Critically Endangered' and placed in the highest category for conservation program attention by the Crocodile Specialist Group (CSG). The CSG has listed three others – the Cuban crocodile, the black caiman, and the gharial – as 'Endangered'. For those species in the Critically Endangered ranks, significant recovery in the wild will be difficult, if not impossible.

The American alligator and its crocodilian kin are the most advanced reptiles.

Crocodilian Facts

American Alligator *Alligator mississippiensis*
Other common names: 'gator

Max size: 19ft 2in (5.8m)
Distribution: SE USA
Reproduction: mound nester; 30–50 eggs
Diet: fish, stingrays, snakes, turtles, herons, nutria, raccoons, deer

Chinese Alligator *Alligator sinensis*
Other common names: T'o, Yow Lung

Max size: 7ft+ (2.2m)
Distribution: lower Yangtze River
Reproduction: mound nester; 10–40 eggs
Diet: snails, clams, fish, rodents

Spectacled Caiman *Caiman crocodilus*
Other common names: common caiman, baba, babilla, jacare tinga

Max size: 10ft (3m)
Distribution: S Mexico to Peru and Brazil; introduced to S Florida, Cuba, Puerto Rico
Reproduction: mound nester; 15–40 eggs
Diet: crabs, snails, fish

Yacare Caiman *Caiman yacare*
Other common names: Jacare, Lagarto

Max size: 10ft (3m)
Distribution: Same as closely related *C. crocodilus*. Feral caimans, mostly escaped or released pets, are found in drainage canals in south Florida.

Broad-snouted Caiman *Caiman latirostris*
Other common names: Jacare overo, Jacare de papo amarelo

Max size: 11ft 6in (3.5m)
Distribution: N Argentina, Bolivia, SE Brazil, Paraguay and Uruguay
Reproduction: mound nester; 20–60 eggs
Diet: molluscs, crustaceans, insects, small vertebrates

Black Caiman *Melanosuchus niger*
Other common names: Jacare assu, Jacare negro, Cocodrillo

Max size: 20ft (6m)
Distribution: Amazon River basin, Guianas
Reproduction: mound nester; ave. 39 eggs
Diet: fish, reptiles including other caiman, capybara

Beauty and the Beast. A basking yacare caiman provides a predator-proof basking spot for butterflies.

Dwarf Caiman *Paleosuchus palpebrosus*
Other common names: Cuvier's smooth-fronted caiman, Jacare pagua, cachirre

Max size: 5ft 6in (1.7m)
Distribution: From Amazon to Orinoco river drainages
Reproduction: mound nester; 10–15 eggs
Diet: invertebrates, fish, and small vertebrates

Smooth-fronted Caiman *Paleosuchus trigonatus*
Other common names: Schneider's smooth-fronted caiman, Jacare coroa

Max size: 7ft 6in (2.3 m)
Distribution : Amazon and Orinoco basins, Guianas
Reproduction: mound nester; 10–15 eggs
Diet: snakes, lizards, birds, porcupines, pacas

American Crocodile *Crocodylus acutus*
Other common names: Cocodrilo, Lagarto, Caiman de la costa

Max size: 20ft+ (6m+)
Distribution: S tip of Florida, to northern S America
Reproduction: hole nester except in poorly drained areas; 30–60 eggs
Diet: fish, turtles, birds, mammals

Orinoco Crocodile *Crocodylus intermedius*
Other common names: Caiman del Orinoco

Max size: 20ft+ (6m+)
Distribution: middle and lower reaches of Orinoco River in Venezuela and Colombia
Reproduction: hole nester in sandbars and river-banks; 40–70 eggs
Diet: poorly known; fish, birds, mammals

Morelet's Crocodile *Crocodylus moreletii*
Other common names: alligator, Cocodrilo de pantano

Max size: 11ft 6in (3.5m)
Distribution: Atlantic coast of Mexico, Guatemala, Belize
Reproduction: mound nester; 20–40 eggs
Diet: snails, fish, turtles, small mammals

Cuban Crocodile *Crocodylus rhombifer*
Other common names: Cocodrilo, Criollo

Max size: 11ft 6in (3.5m)
Distribution: Cuba, Isle of Pines
Reproduction: mound nester; 25–40 eggs
Diet: fish, turtles, birds, small mammals

Nile Crocodile *Crocodylus niloticus*

Other common names: Mamba, African croc, Madagascar croc, flat dog

Max size: 20ft+ (6m+)

Distribution: Sub-Saharan Africa, Madagascar

Reproduction: hole nester in sandy banks; 16–80 eggs

Diet: fish, antelope, warthogs, zebra, cattle, man

Slender-snouted Crocodile *Crocodylus cataphractus*

Other common names: African gavial, African sharp-snouted croc

Max size: 13ft (4m)

Distribution: western and central Africa

Reproduction: mound nester; 13–27 eggs

Diet: crabs, fish, frogs, snakes

Dwarf Crocodile *Osteolaemus tetraspis*

Other common names: broad-nosed crocodile

Max size: 6ft 6in (2m)

Distribution: tropical lowlands of central and west Africa

Reproduction: mound nester; 11–17 eggs in captivity

Diet: crabs, frogs, fish

Mugger Crocodile *Crocodylus palustris*

Other common names: marsh crocodile

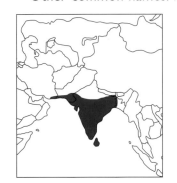

Max size: 13ft (4m)

Distribution: Bangladesh, Iran, India, Nepal, Pakistan, Sri Lanka

Reproduction: hole nester; 25–30 eggs, often double-clutches in captivity

Diet: fish, frogs, snakes, birds, mammals including deer and water buffalo

Siamese Crocodile *Crocodylus siamensis*

Other common names: Buaya kodok, Jara Kaenum-chued

Max size: 13ft (4m)

Distribution: Thailand, Cambodia, Vietnam, Indonesia, Laos, Malaysia

Reproduction: mound nester; 20–50 eggs

Diet: fish and other small vertebrates

New Guinea Crocodile *Crocodylus novaeguineae*

Other common names: Buaya air tawar, Pukpuk

Max size: 11ft 6in (3.5m)

Distribution: Irian Jaya, Papua New Guinea

Reproduction: mound nester; 20–40 eggs

Diet: frogs, fish, reptiles, birds

Philippine Crocodile *Crocodylus mindorensis*
   Other common names: Mindoro crocodile

Max size: 10ft (3m)
Distribution: small isolated populations in Mindanao, Negros, and Mindoro
Reproduction: captives lay 10–20 eggs
Diet: poorly studied; presumably fish, frogs, reptiles, mammals

Australian Freshwater Crocodile *Crocodylus johnsoni*
   Other common names: Johnston's crocodile, 'freshie'

Max size: 10ft (4m)
Distribution: tropical northern Australia
Reproduction: hole nester in sandbars; average 13 eggs
Diet: insects, crustaceans, fish, reptiles, birds, small mammals

Saltwater Crocodile *Crocodylus porosus*
   Other common names: Estuarine crocodile, 'salty', Buaya muara, Pukpuk, Indopacific croc

Max size: 23ft (7m)
Distribution: Tropical Asia and the Pacific from S India to Solomon Islands
Reproduction: mound nester; 40–60 eggs
Diet: large fish, birds, mammals including man

Gharial *Gavialis gangeticus*
   Other common names: gavial

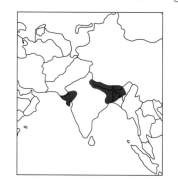

Max size: 20ft+ (6m+)
Distribution: India, Nepal, Pakistan
Reproduction: hole nester in river sandbanks; 30–50 eggs
Diet: fish

False Gharial *Tomistoma schlegelii*
   Other common names: Buaya sumpit, Takong

Max size: 16ft 6in (5m)
Distribution: Sumatra, Borneo, Malay Peninsula, Thailand
Reproduction: mound nester; 20–60 eggs
Diet: fish and small vertebrates

Conservation Status of Crocodilians

Convention on the Trade in Endangered Species of Wild Fauna and Flora (CITES). Appendix I includes species currently threatened with extinction; no commercial activity permitted. Appendix II species not currently threatened with extinction but may become so unless their trade is regulated. Regulations to force the 100+ party nations to enforce CITES took effect in May 1977.

The United States Endangered Species Act (ESA) of 1973. Passed to prevent the extinction of animals and plants by providing measures to help alleviate the loss of species and their habitats. E: endangered species, in danger of extinction. T: threatened species, likely to become endangered within the foreseeable future.

IUCN 1996 Red List of Threatened Animals. Evaluation of threatened status of species by international specialist groups using criteria developed by the International Union for the Conservation of Nature and Natural Resources. Those listed as CR (critically endangered) are considered to have the highest priority for action. EN: endangered; VU: vulnerable; DD: data deficient to fully evaluate threatened status; LR: low risk of extinction.

Family Alligatoridae

	CITES	ESA	IUCN
American alligator, *Alligator mississippiensis*	II	T	LR
Chinese alligator, *Alligator sinensis*	I+II	E	CR
Spectacled caiman, *Caiman crocodilus*	II		LR
Broad-snouted caiman, *Caiman latirostris*	I	E	LR
Yacare caiman, *Caiman yacare*	II	E	LR
Black caiman, *Melanosuchus niger*	I+II	E	EN
Dwarf caiman, *Paleosuchus palpebrosus*	II		LR
Smooth-fronted caiman, *Paleosuchus trigonatus*	II		LR

Family Gavialidae

	CITES	ESA	IUCN
Gharial, *Gavialis gangeticus*	I	E	EN
False gharial, *Tomistoma schlegelii*	I	E	DD

Family Crocodylidae

	CITES	ESA	IUCN
American crocodile, *Crococylus acutus*	I	E	VU
Slender-snouted crocodile, *Crocodylus cataphractus*	I	E	DD
Orinoco, crocodile, *Crocodylus intermedius*	I	E	CR
Australian freshwater crocodile, *Crocodylus johnsoni*	II		LR
Philippine crocodile, *Crocodylus mindorensis*	I	E	CR
Morelet's crocodile, *Crocodylus moreletii*	I	E	DD
Nile crocodile, *Crocodylus niloticus*	I+II	T	LR
New Guinea crocodile, *Crocodylus novaeguineae*	II		LR
Mugger crocodile, *Crocodylus palustris*	I	E	VU
Saltwater crocodile, *Crocodylus porosus*	I+II	E	LR
Cuban crocodile, *Crocodylus rhombifer*	I	E	EN
Siamese crocodile, *Crocodylus siamensis*	I	E	CR
Dwarf crocodile, *Osteolaemus tetraspis*	I	E	VU

Recommended Reading

Graham, A. & Beard, P., *Eyelids of Morning: The Mingled Destinies of Crocodiles and Men,* A&W Visual Library, New York, 1973.

Guggisberg, C.A.W. , *Crocodiles: Their Natural History, Folklore and Conservation,* Stackpole Books, Harrisburg, Pennsylvania, 1972.

Lang, J. W. & Garrick, L. D., *Social Signals and Behaviors of Adult Alligators and Crocodiles,* American Zoologist 17 (1):225-239, 1977.

Neill, W. T., *The Last of the Ruling Reptiles: Alligators, Crocodiles and their Kin*, Columbia University Press, New York, 1971.

Pooley, A. C. & Gans, C., *The Nile Crocodile*, Scientific American 234(4):114-124, 1976.

Ross, C. A., (cons. ed.), *Crocodiles and Alligators*, Merehurst Press, London, 1989.

Steel, R., *Crocodiles*, Christopher Helm, London, 1989.

Webb, G. J.S., Manolis, C. S., & Whitehead, P. J., *Wildlife Management: Crocodiles and Alligators*, Surrey Beatty, Sydney, 1987.

Index

Entries in bold indicate pictures

Biographical Note

John Behler and his wife, Deborah, have worked at the Wildlife Conservation Society since 1970. John is Curator of the Department of Herpetology and Species Coordinator for the Chinese Alligator Species Survival Plan of the American Association of Zoos and Aquariums. Through the UNDP, he helped establish a conservation and management program for Papua New Guinea crocodiles. John is senior author of the Audubon Society Fieldguide to North American Reptiles and Amphibians. He serves as chairman of the IUCN Tortoise and Freshwater Turtle Specialist Group. In recent years he has studied spotted turtles in New York state and the endangered flat-tailed tortoise in western Madagascar. Deborah is Executive Editor of *Wildlife Conservation* magazine. She was secretary to the first IUCN/SSC Crocodile Specialist Group and served as assistant to the group's chairman for many years.